Last Communion

Susan Molyneaux

Northshore Noir

Northshore Noir Press

Northshore Noir Press
Toronto, Canada
www.northshorenoir.com

ISBN: 978-1-998648-09-2

For more information visit: www.northshorenoir.com

For Sylvia—

who taught me how to fuck the page
until it bled perfect metaphor

Contents

POISONED PROMISE

Garden Of Fatal Promises

Through poison-garden nights, they wither—

love's petals rotting in mercury light

while my carmined mouth drips confessions

onto tear-salted sheets. Each promise

I plant takes root in desperate souls,

blooming black beneath their skin.

Fog coils like spent cigarette smoke

through this cemetery of conquered hearts.

My stilettos pierce wet earth like stakes,

marking graves of fools who drank

sweet venom from my silver tongue,

mistaking cobra-sway for grace.

Under corpse-light moon, I cultivate

my deadly bower: curves like nightshade,

words like belladonna berries crushed

between willing lips. Their lust feeds

my garden, each betrayal sprouting

thorns sharp as broken vows.

Watch how hope withers on my vine,

nourished by midnight's keening choir—

these lovers, preserved like pressed flowers

between pages of my black grimoire,

forever kneeling at my thorned throne,

crowned in roses, drowning in lies.

Requiem In Stone

Through ancient stone, dawn breaks like guillotines—

shattering truths into glittering shards.

Mist writhes like funeral shrouds

through marble bones where death's

masquerade spins eternal, their silk-gloved

hands still sticky with my essence.

I track their ritual through morgue-cold

grass, my severed soul in marble pools

ripples like last rites unspoken. They

harvested more than breath that night; they

flayed the flesh that housed my ghost.

Now I'm death's bride, a spectral warning,

dancing through temples of murdered gods.

Shadows swallow confessions whole while

stone devours my mourner's hymn. But in

this fog of sacred slaughter, their secrets

fester in my phantom flesh—

each scar a confession to their betrayal,

each wound a witness that won't stay buried.

Forged In Betrayal

Dawn splinters like crematorium bones
across this necropolis of trust. My
carbonised flesh remembers her inferno—
how she sculpted me with kerosene caresses,
rendered fat to holy water, skin to ash.

Paenitemini, et credite in lapsum.

In this cathedral of char, I genuflect before
altars of collapsed beams, where sanctuary
transmuted to abattoir.

Through neurons

crackling like kindling, I wade through

aftermath and appetite. Her kisses,

phosphorus-white, branded vertebrae like

cattle, until I emerged her masterwork of

blistered redemption.

But from this ossuary of innocence, I rise—

not phoenix, but furnace, each scar a

burning tribute. Watch how morning gilds

my wounds with molten prophecy; my body

now cartography of survival, each keloid a

medal pinned by hell's own hands.

Witness how I forge armour from ashes,

hammer vengeance from melted chains. She

meant to render me to incense, instead I've

become the conflagration—my scars now

burning like demon-blessed rubies,

cauterising her ghost from memory's flesh.

Smoke And Silk

I weave myself in treachery's finest silk,

stitching falsehoods with a widow's precision

into the knowing wound of my crimson mouth.

Watch me glide through electric darkness,

my hips writing serpentine prophecies

while midnight hungers pulse beneath flesh.

They're blind to the asp coiled within

this sainted mask of rouge and shadow,

how I harvest their paper hearts

and slowly drain faith's sweet wine.

Each touch a cold equation,

each fevered coupling a sacred betrayal.

Between bitter gin and smoke signals,

I spin deception's gossamer net.

Dumb lambs stumble to my altar,

drunk on the incense of empty prayers.

Their confessions spill like cheap spirits

down my forever-famished throat.

Dawn finds them broken and exposed,

more than innocence desecrated—

wealth bleeds out in crimson streams,

their names now black as winter nights.

While I drift to fresh hunting grounds

wrapped in stolen skins and stories,

a wraith in veils of cigarette smoke

and crystal glasses weeping wine.

Venom And Veritas

Diamond facets splinter light to shards,

Each glint a scalpel in amber depths.

Their gazes dissect me through smoke-thick air,

Blind to the basilisk's long game.

This dress: a flayed skin stretched tissue-thin,

Each sequin a scale that maps my lies.

My hips pendulum like a mortician's watch,

Drawing them deep where oxygen dies.

My lips, red as first-cut arteries.

Rim poison on Waterford crystal's edge.

They surge forward, these silk-collared lambs,

Mistaking my maw for mercy's pledge.

When twilight haemorrhages into dark,

I'll moult this rhinestone epidermis.

Steel parts flesh like biblical truth—

Their lying eyes turn glass in death's kiss.

SACRED PROFANITIES

The Spider's Liturgy

She weaves my autopsy with haemorrhaged hands,

each sinew-thread a promise meant for breaking.

Her loom devours flesh like hungry gods,

spinning terror from my marrow's milk

while daybreak bleeds across her web,

this charnel house of silk and bone.

Watch how my essence unravels—stitch by stitch,

beneath her surgical depravity. Her fingers,

velvet-gloved in false mercy, plunge

through warp of nerve and weft of vein,

perverting sacred flesh to profane art,

each knot a fresh violation blessed.

I feel my fibres splitting at their core,

chromosomes unzipping beneath her touch

while she claims this vivisection holy—

my torment transformed to textile relics.

But I'm dissolving into septic lace,

too gangrenous to hold this mortal coil.

Soon, only raw meat-threads remain,

memory-soaked sinew, spine-string harps

for her to splice into fresh abominations.

My death-rattle harmonises with her loom's

obscene orgasmic moan, while fate

parcels out my final breaths in viral patterns—

dark mutations spreading through her web,

infecting every soul she'll harvest next.

Communion Of The Damned

Gelatin capsules weep their false eucharist

across sanctuary floors—each pill

a tiny casket promising paradise,

while the needle genuflects, its serpent-tongue

delivering chemical absolution to prostrate veins.

Light gags on incense of decay.

In razored mirrors, reality fractures:

track marks bloom like stigmata,

flesh stretched taut across hollowed temples

where dignity was crucified on pleasure's cross.

Each plunger's thrust rewrites scripture

in bruise-ink and desperate devotion,

until memory itself turns prostitute.

These catacomb walls bear witness

as I trade flesh for synthetic grace—

my corpus a debased communion wafer

passed through underground confessionals

beneath fluorescent judgement lights.

My scars chart pilgrim's progress to hell.

Silence metastasizes room to room,

thick with surrender's sweet decay.

Beyond shattered glass, the profane world

spins on while I genuflect before my toxic idol,

universe contracted to this rusted spoon

cradling crystalline stars of damnation.

Midnight Mass

Through smoke-thick air, they dance their death—

teeth gleaming like spent bullet casings

while the siren weaves her web of breath,

each thread perfumed with tomorrow's mourning.

She drinks her poison like cheap champagne,

drunk on the prophecy of her skin.

Neon bleeds across their ritual,

painting stigmata on writhing limbs.

Their tango writhes serpentine,

crystal stems snapping like small bones

while her mascara runs like crude oil,

marking territory with a predator's smile.

Silver whispers between silk sheets—

her blade thirsting for communion,

ready to baptize tender veins

in sacraments of crimson.

Poor lamb, so blind to the wolf's mass,

hypnotized by her midnight mass.

I chronicle their last waltz:

how hope fled her trembling heart

while newsprint prophets question why

love's knife cuts arteries apart.

But I saw their sheets turn scarlet,

passion's flame drowning in its flood—

this noir tableau's final act

painted in arterial gouache.

Vespers For The Vanished

In this brutalist basilica of steel and stone,

footfalls toll like funeral bells, each step

an antiphon of conversations haunting

these desecrated halls. Distant sirens keen

their urban requiem—a dirge as intimate

as arterial pulse, as constant as regret.

Dust performs its eucharistic dance

through shafts of martyred light,

chronicling an exodus of souls,

doors sealed like pharaohs' tombs.

I census the negative spaces

where warmth once held communion,

measuring absence in nicotine stigmata

and coffee-stain stations of the cross.

Darkness seeps through fractured windows

like ink through shrouds, painting shadows

where voices once celebrated life.

My fingers trace cold steel veins,

seeking ghost-warmth of ancient steam,

anything to fill this void—this perpetual fall

into my own event horizon of invisibility,

crushed beneath the mass of unwitnessed existence.

Confessions To A Drowning Moon

Salt-stained letters bleed their mortal sins,

baptised in brine and arterial spray.

Each tide delivers fresh damnation—

corpse-messages in barnacled bottles.

The women I devoured, the men I unmade—

their names gargled by carrion gulls

while undertow tongues lap my ankles,

dragging me toward darker sacraments

where waterlogged confessions bloom

like jellyfish among the dead.

In this marine morgue, memories float

through kelp-forests of regret: lipstick

traces on throats, knife-kisses on ribs,

all preserved in salt like ancient sins.

I could let Neptune claim his due,

let guilt anchor me to coral graves.

Yet here I persist, tumescent with shame,

fingering love notes turned death warrants.

The shoreline keeps our covenant,

while I collect broken shells like skulls,

counting kills in calcium fragments—

each shard a ledger of my damnation.

Communion Of The Black Widow

In this votive-lit confessional,

I weave fatal liturgies—

fishnets concealing assassin steel beneath,

tongue parsing Merlot and prophesied screams.

My prey trembles under synthetic lashes,

already undone by spectral seduction.

I'll cocoon them in their own desperate yearning,

watch mascara bleed obsidian rivers down cheeks

feverish with forbidden hunger.

Their carotids pulse beneath my crimson altar,

as I map mortality with lacquered omens.

Each sob a sacred symphony,

while I peel flesh like blood-soaked vestments.

Ruby beads consecrate black lace and dermis—

my fingers performing death's intimate waltz through slick
hollows

until rapture erupts in vermilion communion.

Dawn's inquisition pierces night's shroud

as I make my exodus—

leaving them emptied,

exquisitely defiled,

transformed to baroque sculptures of terminal desire.

Their diminishing chorus still echoes,

married to splintering bone and ragged prayers—

my signature in gleaming ichor on silk cerements.

Theatre Of Cruelties

In shadowed wings, I paint my harlot's armour—

rouge mixed from fresh arterial confessions,

my mouth a wound promising sacred violations

I'll withhold like a sadist's sacrament.

The spotlight hungers, a voyeur's eye

famished for tonight's exquisite frauds.

Beneath couture darkness, I count heartbeats

like rosary beads, each pulse a prayer

to false gods of theatrical deception.

These front-row matrons, clutching pearls

under their hems, think they've decoded

the cipher of my manufactured soul.

Vapid cunts. So easily seduced by

porcelain masks and honeyed venom.

My second skin slides on like lingerie,

midnight's most intimate violation.

I've worn this facade of grace so long

my birth-flesh feels like borrowed clothes.

But underneath, authentic darkness writhes—

ophidian hunger with obsidian fangs,

coiled to pierce their willing arteries.

Watch them writhe in velvet seats,

gorging on my crafted agony,

too blind to see how these hands tremble

not from grief but throttled ecstasy,

each glycerin tear a poison seed

sprouting in their fertile trust.

Every martyred virgin I embody

draws me closer to my unholy communion:

their souls spread before me like a feast,

begging for salvation as I consume

their essence, bite by exquisite bite—

the most beautiful monster they'll ever worship,

the last face they'll see before damnation.

CLINICAL
DARKNESS

Death's Courtesan

Through fluorescent purgatory I crawl,

each pulse a mortician's mallet in my skull.

Her venom colonizes failing arteries—

that terminal coitus, that assassin's kiss—

while nurses document my dissolution

in clinical choreography of doom.

My haemorrhaging pilgrimage leaves trails,

viscera liquefying, synapses immolating.

I taste her victory on my tongue,

more lethal than morphine's false mercy.

These letters sear my pocket like acid truth,

secrets I'll carry into oblivion.

My epidermis: cartography of ruin,

death blooming like bruises beneath,

while she reigns victorious in this

terminal tango of flesh and venom.

Her calculation perfect as a surgeon's blade,

her revenge exquisite as cyanide.

I'd genuflect before her lethal altar,

but my throat's too rich with crimson tribute.

Lipstick Autopsy

Through carcinogenic haze and crystalline deceit,

I lacquer my labium in coagulated promises—

each smile a cocked syringe, while her diamond

refracts light like surgical steel against femoral flesh.

Between ethanol solutions and aged Swietenia,

fog compresses dense as tumorous desire,

weighted like morgue-guilt against double-paned glass.

She thinks she's dissecting me, this collector

of formaldehyde lovers and ossified smiles.

Our oral collision splits atoms—

her tongue excavates secrets I've cultured for months.

My carmine marks collar, carotid, and radius,

future forensics in hemoglobin shade,

while her hands chart my epidermis.

She'll diagnose too late: each moan

a calculated chemical reaction,

every touch a practised procedure.

My scalpel parts Valentino silk from fascia—

one final crimson transfusion to complete

my terminal manuscript.

These final verses, fevered testimony,

splash across pages like arterial spray—

while monitors conduct my requiem,

counting down to ultimate ecstasy.

She knew I'd expire still worshipping,

my executioner, my dawn-lit whore,

this body her finest assassination yet.

The Seamstress Of Inevitability

Between industrial bobbins of midnight,

my haemoglobin-crusted digits chart destiny's pattern—

each filament a twisted prognosis,

each ligature where autonomy deliquesces

like virginity in India ink. The loom's teeth

masticate hope like broken jawbones,

counting down my cellular decay.

Auguries emerge in plasma-soaked textile:

Terminal spelled in corpuscular crimson,

in metastasising shadows.

I've watched my prognosis unravel beneath mercury-vapour prophecies,

while scalpel edges phosphoresce

like Lucifer's cataracts.

Night suppurates through window mesh

as each shuttle-thrust sutures my burial

garment in cancerous black. I diagnose this

familiar pathology—so many porcelain

casualties preceded me, watching mortality's

pattern complete itself with surgical precision.

Evisceration Waltz

Through haemorrhaging neon veils,

I glimpse her lethal choreography—

how precisely she strips my essence,

while beneath, her demon's rictus gleams

like surgical steel caressing arteries.

Each shattered pane reflects

my systematic undoing—

a gallery of exquisite violation.

She vivisects me by increments,

defiling me before voyeur windows:

psyche, voice, sanity becoming

props in her grotesque theatre.

Her scalpel maps my topography

while that forked tongue explores

the scarlet atlas of my dissolution.

Soon nothing remains but a hollowed vessel,

splayed and weeping vital essence

onto rain-slicked urban altars.

She'll pirouette with my shell in noir lace,

discard this husk baptised in viscera—

while I keen voiceless, flensed raw,

another conquest in her collection,

trophy in her carnal museum.

Terminal Intimacy Protocol

In this chamber where umbra performs

cellular fusion, scalpels gleam with promises

of surgical invasion, each curve a siren's

frequency calibrated for trauma, saturated in

narcotic aromatics, saccharine molecules

colliding with ferrous haemoglobin.

Desire suppurates like dehiscent tissue,

a collagen filament, tensile, unruptured,

lust's plasma smeared at thirty-seven degrees,

while darkness performs gynaecological genuflection,

each respiratory spasm a countdown to cardiac arrest,

each tachycardic pulse a lancet poised for thoracic penetration.

She traverses mercury-vapour wavelengths,

silhouette excised from pathology's keenest edge,

orbital cavities like quantum singularities,

consuming photons and serotonin,

an invitation inscribed in cicatricial tissue

and primitive hypothalamic impulses—

a protocol where lethal intimacy induces

hypoxic euphoria.

None emerge from her terminal examination

unvivisected; the stimulus, a neural death-rattle,

the precise incision between pleasure and trauma—

in her laboratory,

exsanguination yields violent entropy.

Ethanol Autopsy

Crystalline structures deliquesce in my
terminal solution, each fractured teardrop
diluting synaptic archives of haemoglobin-
stained labia and lethal contracts. I should
have diagnosed when your kiss turned
septic—mortality wears multiple dermis,
yours the most necrotizing.

Limbic echoes infect amber penumbra,

primitive frequencies from initial

contamination, when your pheromones

cauterised neural pathways, branded

hippocampus. Now your toxins traverse

those same compromised axons.

Fluorescent filaments flutter like cardiac

arrhythmia, while my contaminated beaker

cradles pathologies you'll take to an

unmarked ossuary. In terminus, our

malignant passions and metastasised verities

dissolve in one final caustic absorption.

Pyrolysis Of Intimacy

Combustion patterns oscillate like neural misfires

through relationship's necrotic debris.

Tonight, I wear your calcined remains

like latex surgical precision.

In each severed synaptic bond,

fresh oxidation reactions ignite,

consuming our shared cellular structure

in electrochemical warfare.

Through rain-slicked urban arteries,

I leave my haemoglobin signature—

each betrayal a forensic tableau

of pathological artistry exposed.

My metacarpals, scalpel-sharp, incise

epidermis: my laboratory substrate,

until your plasma flows at body temperature,

and I analyse your vocal cord spasms.

Watch me catalyse these endothermic reactions,

calibrating instruments to your terminal frequencies.

Surgical Genesis

Under fluorescent confessionals,

they strip me raw—canvas for steel psalms.

Each cut whispers transformation's creed

while white-robed priests trade clinical prayers

and glass chalices await communion.

Solutions promise sacred rebirth,

ice-bright baptism through altered veins—

each drop dissolving what made me human,

distilling heartbeats to pure data,

archived beneath surgical lights

where sweat and Betadine paint icons.

Do you see me dissolving? A ghost

in this cathedral of gleaming steel,

lost in liturgies of precise incision

where metamorphosis preaches heresy,

and I am merely the sacrifice,

an offering to science's cold gods.

Tonight, they sustain this mortal clay

only to reshape divine creation,

stretching identity's boundaries

like skin across surgical doctrine,

while antiseptic censers swing,

and monitors chant their binary vespers.

Hush, Specimen

At my symposium of calculated terminus,

I serve revenge on surgical steel.

My lover-specimen reclines, trusting,

sipping cyanide from Waterford stems—

each toxic kiss accelerating

cellular death between us.

She vivisects herself, peeling back dermis,

blind to the sepsis in my smile.

My phalanges map her consenting flesh,

charting incision trajectories.

I palpate her carotid architecture,

count diminishing systolic rhythms.

Watch her arch in terminal rapture,

spine contorting on Egyptian cotton,

while my free hand finds cold titanium

nested in medical gauze.

One precise thrust will silence her frequency,

leave her pupils fixed and dilated.

"Why?" she'll aspirate through haemoglobin.

I'll sample the query from her lips,

analyse the ferrous betrayal flowing.

"Hush, specimen," I'll whisper.

"Some procedures exceed romance.

This was always your prognosis."

I'll observe as brain death blooms,

cradle her against my sternum.

Silk darkening to oxidised crimson.

Our final chemical reaction.

Synapses severed absolutely

by love's most clinical incision.

Forensic Recompense

Tonight, photographic plates weep

chemical confessions—evidence saturated

in pheromones and cordite residue,

each exposure a ballistic trajectory targeting

empire's necrotic core.

Your dermal whorls contaminate these

pathological archives, like the disarticulated

specimens you presumed interred.

Through urban capillaries slick with

degeneracy, I bear retribution, precise as

surgical steel, cold as terminal cyanosis.

You constructed your dynasty on ruptured

hymens and haemoglobin pacts, but Themis

now performs my laboratory protocols,

balancing ledgers in carmine pigments and arterial spray.

Some debts demand payment in excised tissue—

this axiom learned beneath your clinical weight.

Now each fraudulent document bearing your

signature transforms to ligature around your

trachea, while I extract compensation,

compounded with necrosis.

Mercury vapour oscillates like Lucifer's strobing laboratory above this amphitheatre of terminal accountability.

They'll discover your specimen displayed by aurora, arranged in meticulous anatomical presentation: the masterwork of gynaecological vengeance, rendered in the spectrum of your every violation, preserved in monochromatic perpetuity.

URBAN HUNTERS

Nocturne For A Dead Detective

Shadows fuck brick walls like guilty fingers,

while I catalog her blood-wealth splashed on

Carrara marble—an obscene baptism of

crimson and greed.

Three weeks deep in death's ledger, and

these shadows hold more truth than my

badge—voyeurs to her finale, when stiletto

steel rewrote her corrupt gospel, etching

confessions into cooling flesh.

Rain carries copper communion down storm drains,

past evidence I missed while chasing neon mirages,

my ethics bent like a whore's morality.

Precinct wolves whisper: green detective,

too soft for death's intimacies.

But they never saw those eyes—how shadows

pooled there like spent morphine dreams,

dark as a pimp's redemption, permanent

as track marks in virgin veins.

My shadow stretches, merges with night's congregation—

those that witnessed, those that killed,

this dark orgy of deceit prowling

our perpetual purgatory.

While lust and death perform their ritual waltz

beneath haemorrhaging neon, prophylactics litter

sacred alleys like fallen angels. I chase phantoms,

fighting desires that promise damnation,

knowing each shadow harbors devils

hungry for another detective's soul.

Symphony Of Lead And Lipstick

Dawn splits the sky like brass-knuckled judgment,

cracking night's protection racket over gutted streets.

From my voyeur's perch—where nicotine

and bottom-shelf bourbon pickle my

conscience—I trace her liberation: crushed

stemware, arterial constellations,

lingerie landmines.

Three stories up, a window gapes obscenely,

curtains snapping like dominatrix's leather.

Chrome handcuffs kiss the radiator, still slick

with animal negotiations—oxidized steel

on velvet flesh chronicles her desperate tango,

each chain link a rosary of resistance.

She paid her exodus in locksmith's craft

and hollow points. Morning air marinates

in cordite perfume and predator's pride,

while this concrete jungle bares its decay

in a mortician's knowing smirk.

Through needle-strewn alleys, her getaway

carves rebellion in rubber and asphalt.

She's napalmed her circus of needle-sharp

promises, her cage of chemical dreams

and flesh merchants. Left her captors

sprawled like fallen kings, marinating

in their own putrid redemption.

Darkness hemorrhages from exit wounds

while she brandishes her defiance

like a stiletto at god's throat,

strutting into genocide sunrise,

phoenix-fierce and prison-proven.

Undercover Nocturne

In this city where neon devours shadow,

Where stilettos drill holes in midnight's membrane,

I decode their venomous liturgies—

Their serpentine sigils, their terminal strains.

Trust is currency in this gangrenous realm,

Where commerce thrives on rotting dreams.

I mint counterfeit faith with practiced hands

While they ink blood-pacts on concrete screens.

Heat writhes down vertebrae like brass knuckles,

While bass lines pound confessions raw,

Too profane for any priest's absolution

(Some sins taste sweeter when they gnaw).

Each cipher bleeds its story of want:

Protection rackets paid in marrow,

Covenants sealed in needle-punctured veins,

Treachery carved in skull and arrow.

Trust is currency in this noir-soaked hell,

And tonight I'm raiding their diseased vault—

Badge nestled between sequin and bone,

Ready to crack their empire's fatal fault.

Confession At The Terminal Diner

Across blood-flecked Formica, her hands flutter

like moths trapped in formaldehyde.

Nicotine fog sutures the space between us

while urban gangrene presses window glass—

voyeuristic tumors hungry for decay.

"Detective," she hemorrhages, mascara

running like sepsis down porcelain features.

"The bastard had it coming." Truth suppurates,

seeps between us like mortified flesh

under fluorescent autopsy lights.

Each confession drops like a coronary,

words ricochet off steel tables, hollow bone.

His fractured chronometer counts in my pocket,

metronomic death-rattle for her liturgy—

cleaver-flash, alley-mouth, muffled surgical screams

beneath the city's cancerous percussion.

I watch her carmined fingertips orbit

ceramic's broken edge, leaving spirals

like those etched in wooden handle-grain,

DNA whorls of desire and disgust.

Patient Zero

In this metropolis, my cultures bloom
beneath fluorescent microscopes of night—
each streetlight a scalpel marking fresh
contamination, while I proliferate through
concrete veins.

Watch how beautifully systems fail: immune
responses choke on protocol, while I breach
membrane after membrane, dancing past
their sterilized defenses like a ballerina
through glass.

I colonize their sterile institutions, multiply
in bureaucratic blind spots, each new
mutation more elegant—(such exquisite
violence in adaptive resistance).

Through lymphatic alleys I disperse, coding
fresh vectors in my wake. Their antibodies
wear brass badges: obsolete metal against
my shifting strain.

Cell by cell, I corrupt their corpus: first
responders fall to fever dreams, while
officials drown in viral load—each death a
perfect, pristine petri dish.

Soon the whole city runs septic, its organs failing in synchronous collapse. They never knew their patient zero wore a lab coat, carried a badge, and smiled.

Now I prepare for wider dispersion, my spores eager for virgin territory. Watch neighboring cities' lights flicker while I multiply in their blind spots the original strain they failed to contain.

Mirror Hunter

Evidence spreads like fallen angels,

each print a dark communion—

rouge-stained flesh and open wounds,

silk nooses kissing marble throats.

I chase her ghost through midnight streets,

smoke burning like mourner's tears.

Behind each broken offering she leaves.

I read her signature in scarlet:

How she guides them into darkness,

ecstasy frozen on lifeless faces.

Their arranged forms map her pilgrimage

through perfumed rooms and strangled prayers.

Truth builds in terrible beauty:

garnets gleaned from her cruel nails,

pearl-shine painted on cold skin,

portraits of their final surrender.

Each frame drips with dark desire,

drawing me toward her velvet snare.

Tonight I'll catch her sacred dance,

witness her ritual of ruin and rapture.

But as I reach to seize her wrist,

she turns—my reflection bares its teeth.

We're one soul split like rotting fruit,

predator and prey, ecstasy and agony.

Night Hunter's Liturgy

Strobe lights dissect the black mirror floor

where I prowl in arterial lace,

heels striking death's precise meter.

Moths drunk on designer poison stumble

into the web between my thighs.

These painted talons will drip

with vintages darker than wine.

Bass reverberates like opened veins,

ancient and raw beneath the skin.

My diamond collar signals warnings,

sharp as the steel concealed in silk.

Champagne bubbles mask the taste

of fatal kisses, of poisoned contracts.

They miss the spider's cruel smile

behind these glitter-dark eyes.

Watch me dance alone in shadows,

my shade thrown monstrous on walls.

Each sway a trap, each step a grave,

my curves scribing doom's calligraphy.

Tonight I'll string their hearts like beads,

wear their suffering as my crown.

Tiles drink deep these scarlet offerings

while I pirouette through wreckage.

Bodies will decorate my chamber,

trophies of this savage communion.

I'll bathe naked in their essence,

ecstatic to their dying hymns.

Velvet and violence, a lethal draft

I swallow whole, uncut with mercy.

The dame is death's own daughter,

her beauty leaves only corpses cold.

Haute Predation

Beneath Versace and calcified pearls,

my pathology seeps like septic wounds—

melanotic secrets staining epidermis,

while Dom Pérignon effervescence masks

the ferrous bouquet of pending trauma.

I force-feed them my crafted toxins:

society's porcelain automaton,

each laugh a carefully titrated poison.

Behind Christian Louboutin's crimson soles,

parasitic hungers metastasize.

Watch me dissect the bejeweled prey,

trailing pheromones and surgical steel.

They drown in couture delusions,

nerve endings blind to monofilament

severing carotid and consciousness.

Exquisite syncope as they collapse,

aspirating on calculated chemistry.

I'll excise their strata methodically,

sample the treachery beneath fascia,

as they mistake incision for intimacy.

In fluorescent morning's execution,

they'll find my true face debrided—

their viscera adorning Thai silk,

while I stalk more profitable specimens,

wearing their dermis as laboratory coat.

INHERITANCE
OF DARKNESS

Willow's Witness

Beneath the willow's mortuary drape,

I dissected her words like a coroner's prize;

Each promise peeled back like necrotic skin,

While darkness metastasized in my mouth.

Night played anatomist to our theatre,

Cataloging secrets too gangrenous to name.

She pirouetted through her perjuries,

Leaving trust's corpse for carrion birds to claim.

The air coagulated around us, thick

With betrayal's sweet sepsis. I swallowed

Her toxins like aged malt, unsurprised

When each sip crystallized into thorns.

She performed her final arabesque of deceit

Under lunar formaldehyde, while above,

The willow's skeleton fingers transcribed

Our autopsy in trembling chlorophyll.

Maternal Necropolis

Mother's mausoleum exhales malignant memories,

each floorboard keens stillborn secrets beneath my tread.

Shattered crystal charts my pilgrimage like fallen stars,

while heirloom pearls decay where vermin breed.

Portraits hang askew—ancestral tableaux

where smiles split like arsenic-laced communion,

spilling histories viscous as mortician's honey.

Twilight seeps through cataracts of glass,

its septic shadows pooling where we once

played séance with our inherited demons.

August festers with formaldehyde reveries—

preserved specimens of our transgressions float

in mason jar reliquaries, unholy things

that writhe when peripheral vision fails.

I trace her final testament, each syllable

a forensic scar, tomorrow's obituary

gestating in waxen prophecy. Her script

contorts like dying vipers, confessing

in amniotic ink.

Some sins gestate beneath epidermis—

birth themselves in midnight fever-dreams,

like that blade finding its maternal sheath

between her ribs, where truth metamorphoses.

Neon Goddess

Through rain-slick streets where neon bleeds,

I watch her dance, a siren's call,

Each step leaving shattered souls

Like mother's china in her wake.

Her laughter claws against brick walls—

The sound of marriage beds unmade.

Reality warps around her frame

Like flesh beneath my father's belt.

Some nights I see her split apart,

Fragments sharp as wedding rings,

While her claws etch promises

In languages my mother knew.

She writhes between stuttering lights,

Threading death through void's abyss,

Until the rain drowns memory

Like pills in midnight wine.

These streets hold too many truths

For one daughter to endure—

I witness her becoming me,

My skin her second sheath.

Her madness feeds on Sunday hymns,

Corrupting like a mother's lie.

In back alleys, my reflection splits

Where reason's veil grows thin.

She is a goddess of neon and vice,

Ruling the kingdom I couldn't save.

I crave to wear her nightmare now,

To break the way she breaks.

Mad Queen's Consort

Her whispers writhe through rotting walls,

infiltrating my fractured mind

like sweet poison, fatal and divine.

I gorge on her madness, desperate as prayer,

while specters pulse through my veins,

bound to her terrible symphony.

Reason bleeds out in scarlet rivers,

baptizing sterile floors with lost wisdom.

She stripped sanity from my bones,

leaving chaos blooming in the void—

each savage communion a descent

into perfect annihilation.

Now I welcome the darkness within,

let it flood the hollow spaces

where she carved her name in ritual.

My prayers and screams become one voice

as I spiral down her crimson warren,

transforming to match her dark design:

a grotesque psalm of shattered reason,

blessed by her sacred madness.

Broken.

Transfigured.

Eternally damned.

Inheritance Of Venom

Through memory's mausoleum I stalk,

mapping wounds she sculpted in my flesh—

lunar crescents carved by succubus nails,

bruises blooming like midnight orchids

while heritage bleeds into ancient timber,

sins too deep for any baptism to cleanse.

Each chamber throbs with phantom ecstasy,

her voice still coiling like opium smoke—

Circe's song drawing sailors to shipwreck

upon the reef of her porcelain thighs.

Young fool, I drowned in her undertow,

in serpentine embrace and laudanum dreams,

chasing rapture past sanity's shores.

Now tattered silk in gilt-worn frames

conceals the violence of our communion,

while Mother's prophecy echoes true:

some demons wear Venus's mask,

their kisses laced with arsenic grace.

Yet I craved her poison's sacrament,

watched her drink my birthright dry,

consuming legacy and soul alike

in brutal eucharists of flesh,

until nothing remained but crystalline shards

and this desiccated chrysalis she shed—

an empty reliquary of spent desire.

Drowning In Her

In this concrete lake of night,

water licks my ankles like mother's gin breath,

rising with each sin I sold for copper pennies.

The tunnel whispers my collection of crimes—

echoes of drugstore perfume, discount rouge,

and wedding bands I snapped like sparrow necks.

Now waist-deep in rust-warm current, time thickens

like winter's forgotten blood. Her smile splits

wider than my first wife's wrists. I traded truth

for her honey-gilt shrine, my tongue forked

while my sins bred like maggots at my hips,

dragging me down into this sperm-slick dark.

Shoulders, neck—I welcome damnation's tide.

The water tastes of acid rain and dead daughters.

She warned me: the tide keeps its own ledger,

forcing lungs to swallow each stillborn day.

My last breath bubbles up like a whore's prayer

to a goddess who only comes for drowning souls.

Immolation Ritual

In this crematorium city of matchstick men,

I strike myself against their jaws like phosphorus.

Their paper souls catch quick—such thin

skin between pleasure and cremation.

I leave them scattered like father's cigarette ash,

their bodies charred black as mother's wedding dress.

My tongue brands flesh like cattle irons,

marking what I'll later burn away.

Each kiss devours like napalm dreams—

their flesh bubbles beneath my lips

while I feast on screams, Daddy's girl,

burning bridges back to Sunday school.

I am kerosene in silk stockings,

Inferno angel, matchbook madonna.

Watch me birth these bastard flames

until even God turns away, choking.

They beg for death by my burning hand,

these men who smell like father's study.

I'll make them holy through immolation—

every bed my sacrificial pyre.

FINAL SACRAMENTS

Night Sister

The moon bleeds tonight, swollen with want,

while hunger writhes beneath my skin.

Through streets darker than Vantablack,

I taste her terror on the wind.

My shadow uncoils, serpentine,

fangs gleaming behind pearl facade.

Poor prey sees silk and social grace,

blind to the beast that stalks her god.

This crimson light feeds ancient urges

veiled by Chanel and careful lies.

Her screams will paint my midnight mass,

a psalm for those with savage eyes.

They'll blame her death on mindless beasts,

never dreaming monsters wear

French perfume and crimson lips,

designer clothes and coiffed hair.

While my shadow drinks her essence,

the blood moon nods in regal grace—

mother to all midnight daughters

who hunt their sisters' tender face.

We are her get, forever starved,

eternal as the dark we chase.

Night Butcher

Silk whispers like asylum sheets at midnight,

shadows writhe on walls red as mother's lipstick.

My nails chart geographies of madness

across skin mapped with childhood scars—

each pulse a metronome of Catholic guilt.

The air drips sweet as morphine dreams,

coating throats thick as wedding vows.

My hungers eclipse mere flesh-want,

burning deeper than marrow-memory:

midnight's scalpel vivisects desire.

Crimson blooms on virgin cotton,

like first blood on communion dress.

This waltz of wound and weapon—

we dance on surgical steel,

performing sacred mutilations.

In darkness, we paint profane prayers,

sketching hell with haemoglobin ink.

Dawn will find our savage gallery:

torn stockings, spilled rubies,

relics of tonight's exquisite dissection.

They say beauty always draws blood,

but some of us need more than needles—

we crave the final

intimate

incision.

Gallery Of Hunger

Between marble gods and gilt-edged frames,

I prowl with deadly jewels between my thighs—

each step promising exquisite violence,

my dress wound tight as executioner's wire.

Desire's chains draw blood-warm tonight,

while prey drifts through crystal light.

I'll mount them like precious artefacts,

pin still-beating wings to velvet darkness.

Their flesh becomes my finest canvas,

as I paint rapture in living crimson.

Such sweet hymns they'll sing for me.

When bliss transforms to beautiful agony,

watch me writhe in their fading light,

my form possessed by ancient hunger.

I'll drink their essence like dark wine,

feel their pulse flutter and fade

while I harvest their final gasps,

bound eternal to this sacred feast.

These hallowed walls cradle countless souls

I've loved and bled and wrapped in gold.

My collection grows with each dark mass,

every corpse an offering to passion's altar.

Forever prisoner to this burning ritual,

I claim fresh hearts to fill my hollow chest.

Working Girl's Requiem

Forsaken benches collect shadows like her
mother's suicide notes, while mercury vapour
lamps leak ice-blue confessions across
bloodstains we all pretend not to see.

I watched her last Tuesday, seventeen in
stolen stockings, before they found her
splayed like a failed constellation—another
daughter reduced to morgue photographs
and detective's coffee-stained reports.

Winter breeds frost on iron railings, used

needles, her torn lace still caught in thorns

like a communion veil in barbed wire.

The city digests her final prayer in its

concrete stomach, preserving her screams in

formaldehyde streetlight and diesel wind.

Some church lady left dollar-store roses,

petals brown as dried blood—mercy

measured in wilting carnations and semen

crystals on evidence tape.

The Johns migrate like hungry ravens, while

we survivors melt into brick walls, our heels

clicking Morse code warnings to Saint Death.

We paint our lips the colour of emergency

lights, praying we won't join her—another

broken cherub in the city's growing

collection of discarded girls.

Communion Of Pain

Between black satin and surgical steel,

I orchestrate a requiem of opened veins—

each incision precise as a mother's criticism,

each bruise blooming like chapel roses.

Crimson sacrament wells from ivory flesh

while I paint confessions with careful cruelty.

Climax builds in their windpipes like prayer,

my hands conducting their final aria.

They beg in languages learned in convents,

offering bodies like communion wafers.

I drink deep their baptismal screams,

collecting tears in medicine vials.

Splayed on my altar of bone and silk,

they dance like saints in ecstatic fits.

I pierce their hearts with blessed needles,

performing rites of sacred violation.

Their faces freeze in rapture's mask,

while death plays organist to their descent.

I arrange their limbs in cathedral poses,

these martyrs to midnight's medicine.

Each sacrifice feeds my surgeon's hunger,

my scalpel writing psalms in their skin.

Innocence dissolves in formaldehyde dreams—

I leave behind relics for morning's mass.